MW00901636

You Can Be a Friend of God

Discovering the Fruits of the Spirit!

Written By Karen Essenburg

Illustrated by Catherine Clapp

Trilogy Christian Publishers
A Wholly Owned Subsidiary of Trinity Broadcasting Network
2442 Michelle Drive
Tustin, CA 92780

Cover design by: Cornerstone Creative Solutions

For information, address Trilogy Christian Publishing
Rights Department, 2442 Michelle Drive, Tustin, Ca 92780.
Trilogy Christian Publishing/ TBN and colophon are trademarks of Trinity Broadcasting Network.

For information about special discounts for bulk purchases, please contact Trilogy Christian Publishing.

Manufactured in the United States of America

10 9 8 7 6 5 4 3 2 1

Library of Congress Cataloging-in-Publication Data is available.

ISBN 978-1-68556-530-5 (Print Book)
ISBN 978-1-68556-531-2 (ebook)

Note to Parents, Children's Church Teacher, and Young Readers

God is a friend to all who have accepted His Son, Jesus, as their Savior. He desires all His friends to be full of His fruit! When we are full of His fruit, we will be a friend to Him and others!

"But the fruit of the Spirit is love, joy, peace, patience, kindness, goodness, faithfulness, gentleness, self-control..." (Galatians 5:22–23).

You can be a friend of God…When you have God's fruit of *love* in your heart!

Bethany and Noah's daddy had *love* in his heart when he worked all weekend building an outdoor play structure with a fort.

Sophia had *love* in her heart when she stayed all night at the hospital with her grandmother. She gave her grandmother comfort and company after her surgery.

4

Katie had *love* in her heart when she told her mommy, "I really wanted a baby sister, but we can keep him!"

Lovingly, Mommy responded, "We can pray for a sister."

You can be a friend of God...When you have God's fruit of *joy* in your heart!

Aunt Julie had *joy* in her heart when she cooked Thanksgiving dinner and desserts for the family!

Lana and Layla had *joy* in their hearts when they were baptized at Gull Lake Ministries family camp! Papa Mike felt the *joy* and decided to be baptized too!

Landon had *joy* in his heart when he received get-well cards in the mailbox. Many were from people he didn't even know! They wrote, "We are praying you will be well soon!"

12

You can be a friend of God...When you have God's fruit of *peace* in your heart.

Papa Franklin had *peace* in his heart when he played his guitar for Jesus at church with the worship band!

Joey had *peace* in his heart when he forgave his sister for teasing him!

Papa Ralph and Nana Cathie had *peace* in their hearts when they took their grandchildren for a pontoon boat ride! They were thankful for the lake and the beauty God created!

You can be a friend of God…When you have God's fruit of *patience* in your heart!

Olivia had *patience* in her heart when she waited calmly for her daddy to inflate her floating tube.

Michael had *patience* in his heart while he waited for Mr. Rick to dig up worms so they could go fishing! Michael helped carry the fishing poles down to the boat.

Tyler and Wade had *patience* in their hearts when they politely waited in the long line for the roller coaster.

You can be a friend of God…When you have God's fruit of *kindness* in your heart!

Lucas had *kindness* in his heart when he helped his grandmother Lil move to an apartment building!

Patty had *kindness* in her heart when she helped take care of the family pets!

Jenny had *kindness* in her heart when she helped elderly people get dressed and eat their breakfast!

You can be a friend of God...When you have God's fruit of *goodness* in your heart!

Ghada had *goodness* in her heart when she shared her lunch with Rosie. Rosie is a friend at school who accidentally left her lunch box at home.

Brett had *goodness* in his heart when he shared his turtle-hunting skills with David. They paddled out on the lake in canoes and caught turtles to enter the church camp turtle race.

34

Mason had *goodness* in his heart when he helped carry in groceries for his family!

You can be a friend of God…When you have God's fruit of *faithfulness* in your heart!

Gianna had *faithfulness* in her heart when she committed to dancing in the Easter drama. She had to practice her part and attend rehearsals.

Cody and Autumn had *faithfulness* in their hearts when they committed to loving each other. In *faithfulness*, they spoke wedding vows to each other and God.

Jesus had *faithfulness* in His heart when He obeyed His Father and died on the cross for the sins of the whole world. Then He rose again on the third day!

42

You can be a friend of God...When you have God's fruit of *gentleness* in your heart!

Haleigh had *gentleness* in her heart when she gave her baby girl, Evelyn Mae, a warm sponge bath!

Rick and Rob had *gentleness* in their hearts when they helped rescue their sprinting toddler brother from running onto the baseball fields!

Papa Rick had **gentleness** in his heart when he showed Finley how to gently strum the guitar with his pick.

48

You can be a friend of God…When you have God's fruit of *self-control* in your heart!

Katie had *self-control* in her heart when mean boys spoke hurtful words to her. She responded kindly, with brave appropriate words!

Trevor had *self-control* in his heart when he followed instructions at the church Fall Festival party. He only ate one donut when he saw the sign, "One donut per person!"

Teddy had **self-control** when his dad requested, "Stay off the lake until the storm passes by." Teddy respectfully waited to go sailing until the bad weather cleared up.

Would you like to have **God's fruits of the Spirit** in your heart? God's love and all the fruits can live in your heart starting today! Pray this prayer with me.

> *Dear God, I invite Jesus to fill my heart with His love and forgiveness. Please help me to have all the fruits of His Spirit. I receive the gift of Your love for me.*

Thank You for sending Jesus so I can be forgiven, full of love and all the fruits of the Spirit!

Amen!

CPSIA information can be obtained
at www.ICGtesting.com
Printed in the USA
BVHW060029090922
646609BV00001B/1

* 9 7 8 1 6 8 5 5 6 5 3 0 5 *